PROUDLY WE HAIL

Proudly

HOUGHTON MIFFLIN COMPANY • BOSTON

New York   Atlanta   Geneva, Illinois   Dallas   Palo Alto

We Hail

VASHTI BROWN · JACK BROWN

with illustrations by DON MILLER

ABOUT THE AUTHORS

VASHTI BROWN was educated at Fisk University and Hunter College. She has taught reading in both elementary and junior high schools in New York City, and she has served as reading consultant with the New York City Board of Education's Junior High School Reading Project. At present she is a clinical consultant at the Manhattan Reading Center, where she works with students and teachers.

JACK BROWN, who holds two degrees from the College of the City of New York, teaches and serves as chairman of the Social Studies Department at Junior High School 210 in Brooklyn.

DON MILLER was graduated from Cooper Union and studied at the Art Students League. After a varied experience in studios and agencies, he now works as a freelance artist specializing in book illustration.

The authors wish to express their thanks to Margaret Lalor, Junior High School Reading Coordinator for the New York City Board of Education, for technical and literary advice.

For other advice and suggestions the authors are grateful to Rayford W. Logan, Professor of History at Howard University, and to Mrs. Ruby Gillis, Reading Coordinator, Northwestern High School, Detroit.

TO YOU, THE READER

This is your book. It was written just for you. The words are those you know and understand. The stories are not new. They are all true. In fact, they are stories from American history.

Why did we write this book? We wrote it to show how Negroes have a part in the making of America. You can be proud of these men and women. As they gave to America, so can you.

THE AUTHORS

Dedicated to our parents

CONTENTS

The Past

The Present

The Past

These are stories of men and women of times past. Life for them was very hard. The evils done them hurt their pride. The dangers around them made them afraid. But these men and women were not defeated. They let other Americans know what Negroes could do. Their stories are part of the story of America.

Crispus Attucks

Benjamin Banneker

Peter Salem

The Underground Railroad

Harriet Tubman

Henry Box Brown

Jan Matzeliger

Frederick Douglass

Matthew Henson

X

1

What the Bells Told...
CRISPUS ATTUCKS

REWARD for RUNAWAY SLAVE
Crispus Attucks   6 ft. 2 in. tall
new buckskin pants   blue checkered shirt
Signed — William Brown, Framingham, Mass.

Even with this ad in the Boston paper, Crispus Attucks was never caught. He had to be free. So he ran away.

And for twenty years he lived with the terrible fear of beatings, and even death, if they found him. He meant it when he said that he'd rather die than be a slave.

Now, from England, came the fighting Redcoats. The king sent guns and bayonets. The Americans had few arms. The two sides began hating each other. Each side called the other names. Sometimes the soldiers rushed at the Americans with fixed bayonets just to frighten them. But this only made the people more angry.

Just at this time — from somewhere — came Crispus Attucks. He wanted to fight *now* for all Americans to be freed from England. "Are you going to stand for the way the Redcoats are treating you?" he asked the crowd.

"No, no!" they cried out in anger. Thus, he became one of their leaders.

Then, one winter night, a little after nine o'clock, it

happened. Bells began to ring — big bells, little bells, fire bells, cow bells, dinner bells, and church bells — all the bells the people could get hold of. The bells were calling all the men to help fight the Redcoats. The Americans used fists and clubs; the Redcoats used guns and bayonets.

Crispus and a dozen others stood up to the soldiers, ready to fight for their freedom. Shots rang out! One man fell! It was Crispus Attucks. Then four other Americans were shot down. This was the Boston Massacre (MAS-sa-cre). The runaway slave who had to be free was the first American to die in a struggle that led to his country's freedom. Many more like him died in the Revolutionary War that followed.

Someday, when you visit Boston, you will find a monument on Boston Common with the name of Crispus Attucks. It helps us remember him and what he did.

2

School in the Sky...

BENJAMIN BANNEKER

Benjamin Banneker was a boy who used his brain. One day he took a pocket knife and some wood, and he made a clock. He made it so well that it struck the hour and told the time for twenty years.

Ben's father was a slave who was able to buy his own freedom. Because his father was no longer a slave, Ben was born free.

Ben was lucky to be free. He was also lucky to be able to go to school. He went to school long enough to

learn to read and write well. He was a whiz in math. Math was an adventure for him. It was the key to all the great things he was to do.

Before he was fifteen, Ben had to leave school to help his father work on their farm. He hated to leave school. He had not learned all he wanted to. But he had learned that he had a good brain, and for the rest of his life he *used* it.

Ben liked to gaze at the stars and wonder about their movements. He had no telescope (TEL-e-scope) to study the stars. He had no teacher or books. So he made the sky his school.

About this time the Ellicott family built a flour mill near Ben's home in Maryland. Ben became friendly with George Ellicott. They found they were interested in the same things. They watched the stars together. George loaned Ben books to read. They talked about what they had seen in the sky and about what they had read in the books.

Soon Ben could tell how the stars moved. He knew where they would be in the sky at any time of the year. He knew when the moon would look different and he knew why. All this he had learned without a telescope. He learned from just watching the sky.

Ben was fast becoming an astronomer (as-TRON-o-mer). This is a person who knows about stars and planets and can tell what is happening in the sky. It is not easy to become an astronomer. Even if you are lucky enough to be in school, it is hard.

One day Ben and George were talking about the mysteries of the skies. Ben's white friend asked, "Why don't you write an almanac?" An almanac is a book that tells many things, like what the weather will be at different times of the year. To know the weather, you have to study the skies. Farmers need to know about the weather so they can decide when to plant their crops. A book of this kind would be very helpful to them. Ben liked the idea, so he started to write an almanac.

Ben's highest honor came to him while he was writing his almanac. He was asked to help plan the new capital city of the United States. A group of men were planning this city that became Washington, D.C. One of the Ellicotts belonged to this group. He told them about Ben and all the things he could do. They sent for Ben because they needed his help.

One of these city planners, a Frenchman, became angry and went away. He took the plan for the new city away with him. But Benjamin Banneker remembered the plan, and he drew the new city just as he had seen it. Benjamin had worked with wheels for the clock he made long ago. He had watched the wheels that ground the

6

wheat in the Ellicott's flour mill. He had watched the stars move in wheels through the sky. Once again he saw a wheel. The plan for the new capital, Washington, D.C., was shaped like a wheel. It had the big dome of the Capitol as its center. Here is a picture of the plan.

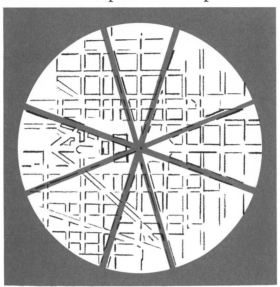

Benjamin returned home, proud to have served his country. He went straight back to his almanac and finished it. It was first printed in Baltimore in 1792. There were few newspapers then, so an almanac was really needed.

The almanac was very useful to farmers. One farmer in Virginia was Thomas Jefferson, who later became President of the United States. He wrote to Benjamin Banneker about the almanac, and Benjamin wrote letters to him. Copies of these letters can be seen in the New York Public Library.

A whiz in math, an astronomer, a writer, a city planner — that was one Negro, Benjamin Banneker! He was a boy who never stopped using his brain.

3

A Shot from the Hill . . .

PETER SALEM

A minute or two was all it took for the Minutemen to get ready to fight. Their guns were poor. They had little training. The British Redcoats had fine guns and a lot of training. They had become the best soldiers in the world. These soldiers had made the Americans so angry they forgot to be afraid. They stood up to the Redcoats.

Now the Americans knew also that they would have to free their slaves. They must use them to fight along with the Minutemen. If they did not, the Redcoats would use them. One of the slaves who went into the American army was Peter Salem. He wanted his country to be free, just as he himself wanted to be free.

Up on a hill, near Boston, a brave little army of Minutemen built a wall. They built it of earth and stones. From behind it, they could fire down on the big army of Redcoats. The general of the Redcoats ordered Major Pitcairn (PIT-cairn) to chase the Americans off that hill. This battle became known as the Battle of Bunker Hill.

Up came the major with his great army of Redcoats. The Americans waited behind the wall. Their arms were old muskets, sticks and stones. "Don't fire until you see the whites of their eyes!" called their leader. They held their fire. The Redcoats got very close. Then came a round of fire. The English fell back. Up they came again. Again the Americans fired. Back fell the Redcoats once more.

Now the powder and bullets of the Americans were getting low. Major Pitcairn knew this. So up the hill, again, he came with his men. This time, Pitcairn jumped on the wall and shouted, "The day is ours!" At that moment Peter Salem took aim and fired. The major fell, killed by Salem's bullet. The death of their leader stopped the Redcoats only for a moment. But in that moment the Americans got away safely into the woods.

Today, in Framingham, Massachusetts, you will find this stone above Peter Salem's grave:

The people of Framingham put the stone at the grave to honor this brave Negro. He was among the first to shed his blood in the American Revolution.

4

Escape ... THE UNDERGROUND RAILROAD

No tracks! No engines! Was this really a railroad? It was called the Underground Railroad because it was kept secret. It was the name used for the way slaves escaped. Many slaves escaped to the free land in the North by using this railroad.

All railroads have stations. The stations of the Underground Railroad were the houses of friends, about ten to fifteen miles apart. This distance was just about a night's trip. Kind people, Negro and white, took slaves into their homes and hid them. Their homes were the stations. This was very dangerous, for if a slave was found in a house, the owner was put in jail.

All railroads have trains to carry people. These trains were wagons, carts, or horses.

All railroads have tracks. Dusty roads, forest paths, and swamps were these tracks. Some slaves went on foot.

All railroads have conductors. Their job is to help people. The Underground had about three thousand of them. Very brave men and women of both races were the conductors on this line. They led the runaway slaves to safety.

How did this Underground Railroad work? A conductor would help a slave escape from his master. The slave would hide under a load of hay, in a cart or in a wagon. He would ride the dusty road to the first house, or station. The owner would hide the slave in his home until he was ready to go on to the next house. He would go from house to house until he came to a free state.

Sometimes, cruel slave-catchers would come and search these homes. These men were paid by the masters to find and bring back the runaway slaves. This was the way they made their living.

Many of the slave-catchers used bloodhounds. But the
runaways knew how to lose them. If they walked in water,
the bloodhounds could not trail them. The slaves found
streams of water wherever possible. They walked for miles
and miles upstream.

Runaway slaves rested and slept during the day. They
hid in caves or graveyards. They slept in barns, corncribs,
cellars, or churches.

Nighttime was for travel. They followed the North
Star. On dark nights they felt the trees. Moss grew on
the north side. So, tree by tree, they headed for freedom.

A coachman's dress fooled many a slave-catcher on the
highway. A slave dressed as a coachman drove a fine
carriage. Inside sat a white man posing as his master.

16

TWO TYPES OF RAILROADS

UNDERGROUND RAILROAD—
ESCAPE FOR THE SLAVE

REGULAR RAILROAD—
TRAVEL FOR THE FREE

STATIONS

TRAINS

CONDUCTORS

TRACKS

TRAVEL

When they reached a safe hiding place, the white rider would drive his carriage home. He was a conductor who had led a slave to freedom.

There were many groups of white people who helped slaves reach freedom. One was a group of church people called Quakers. They dressed differently from other people. Many of them went bravely to jail for doing what they thought was right.

Farmers, too, helped runaways ride the highway. One farmer loaded his wagon with corn. But this was a strange

wagon. It had a false bottom. Slaves hid in this bottom before the corn was piled on top of them. Then the farmer drove north to the market.

No railroad of iron and steel ever took better care of its passengers. No conductors ever loved their riders more. All who rode the Underground looked eagerly to the end of the line — freedom.

5

The General Was a Lady...
HARRIET TUBMAN

A little brown lady was walking fast up the road to our door. So this was the General! I knew it because I saw my mother smile. She had not smiled before, today. She had been saying only that the General was coming. My mother's smile told me that the General's coming meant something good. I knew that soon her secret would be mine, too.

When the little lady came into our cabin, the group of slaves who were there came close to her and stood still. She talked softly to them. "I will lead you to freedom." They all smiled. "It will not be easy. There may be trouble. But there is no turning back. Are you ready?" They were ready.

"This time, you will ride under hay. You will lie on the floor of the wagon. We will cover you with hay. Lie still. Do not talk. In a few hours we will come to our first station. It will be a house where you will be safe. You will eat and rest there. You will be told how and when to go on. Remember, once we start, *there is no turning back.*"

The Little General, Harriet Tubman, wore an ugly mark of slavery. It had been given to her by a cruel master. Harriet had tried to help another slave escape. This angered the master. He threw an iron weight that struck her. The blow made a deep gash on the side of her head.

For days, she knew nothing. Then slowly she recovered. But the deep mark stayed with her. She carried it the rest of her life.

As a result, Harriet had blackout spells. Suddenly, without any warning, she would fall asleep. Just as suddenly, she would wake up. Then all would be well again.

My mother had told me stories about Harriet Tubman — how she used the stopping places on the road to the north. These made up the Underground Railroad. This railroad had no rails. It did not run under the ground. Men and women made up this railroad. Many of them were white. If this way of escape for slaves had been found out by the masters, all who helped would have been put in jail or killed.

Harriet Tubman herself had run away. Her master offered a reward of $40,000 for her capture. No one ever collected it. She made nineteen trips and led three hundred slaves to freedom. Not one of them did the masters catch. Harriet, the conductor, boasted, "I have never lost a passenger."

The Underground way of getting slaves to freedom is one of the great adventure stories of American history. Helping slaves ride the Underground Railroad put many people in great danger. Those people, both Negro and white, who helped the Lady General were very brave.

6

A Quaker Walks By ...

HARRIET TUBMAN

All night long, Harriet Tubman and her band of runaway slaves had been making this trip. Quietly, they had made their plans. Silently, they had met at midnight. Steadily, they had tramped through the dark fields and woods. Just before the light of day, they came to the first station. Leaving the little party hiding in the dark, she gave her signal knock at the door. No answer. She knocked again. At last, a strange white face appeared at the window and called loudly, "Who are you, and what do you want?" Harriet Tubman asked for the friend who always took them in. Again the voice shouted, "Your friend was put in jail for helping runaway slaves."

Here was real trouble! Day was breaking. Slave-hunters would soon be on their trail through the woods. The Little General thought for a moment. Nothing must stop her. *She would free these people.* She remembered that outside

22

this town there was a little island in the swamplands.
Quickly, she led her little band of slaves there. She told
them to lie down in the tall, wet grass. They were to stay
there in the cold and the wet until it was dark. She did
not dare leave them, even to get food. The enemy might
be on their trail. All was quiet now.

Just before dark, a man came walking, very slowly,
along the dry path at the edge of the swamp. They saw
by his dress that he was a Quaker, so they knew he was
their friend. He seemed to be talking softly to himself.
Yet they heard every word he said: "My wagon stands
in the barnyard of the next farm, across the way. The horse
is inside the barn, and the man is gone."

Night fell. Harriet Tubman hurried to the place. What
did she find? Not only were the horse and wagon there
but food as well. She drove the wagon back to the swamp.
How glad they were to get food and a ride to the next
town. They were one step nearer to freedom.

How the good man found out about them in the swamp
Harriet Tubman never knew. She simply said that God
had answered her prayer for help.

7

Man in a Box...

HENRY BOX BROWN

*Your case of goods is shipped and
will arrive early tomorrow morning.*

These words came to Mr. McKim by wireless in Philadelphia. He knew this was a warning from the Underground Railroad. They were sending through another slave. But in a box? And by train?

The slave inside this box was Henry Brown. He had thought up this mad plan for himself. He had run away from his mean master in Virginia. He was told how dangerous his plan was. He said only, "I'd rather die than be a slave."

Into the small box stepped Henry. He would just fit inside if he pulled up his knees close to his chin. A few crackers and a bottle of water were given to him. A gimlet, a tool for making holes, was put in with him too. Then the top was nailed on. Now the poor slave was not able to move. The box was addressed to:

Mr. William McKim
195 Archer Street
Philadelphia, Penna.
THIS SIDE UP WITH CARE

This box would go by express. The express men were not always careful. During some of his twenty-six-hour trip, poor Henry stood on his head.

At last the train pulled into Philadelphia. Mr. McKim was waiting for his passenger. He wondered if he'd be able to move his arms or legs. Would he even be alive!

When he saw the box, he knocked gently. He whispered, "All right?"

"All right, sir," the answer came.

Mr. McKim put the box on his wagon and drove home. When the box was opened, out crept Henry Brown. Slowly, he stood up to his full size. He moved his stiff arms and legs and shook himself. He was happy now. For that broken box from which he stepped was to him the broken chains of slavery. Now he was free.

Mr. McKim was just as happy as Henry. He told him that from now on, he would have a new name. It would be Henry *Box* Brown — for he had come to freedom in a box.

8

A Shoe a Minute...

JAN MATZELIGER

Every boy and girl in the United States should know the boy who did "the impossible." He was Jan Matzeliger (Mat-ZE-li-ger), a Negro. It is because of him that we can buy shoes so cheaply today.

Jan was born in South America. He was only ten when he started to work. His father got him a job in the

26

government machine works. He went for a time as a learner. Before long he handled machinery well.

Later, he spent some time working in his father's machine shop. He liked the tools, the drills and the motors. But he wanted to make money using machinery. So he decided to find work away from home.

He went to Massachusetts. There, he found work in a shoe factory. Older men made the upper parts of shoes and sewed them together by hand. Then Jan sewed the upper parts of the shoes to the soles with a machine. He felt very sorry for these other men. They were older than he, and they worked hard and late. Working by hand was very hard.

"I believe I could make a machine that could do what you are doing," he told them. Of course, they laughed at him. They told him it was impossible. To make shoes, a machine needed fingers like theirs.

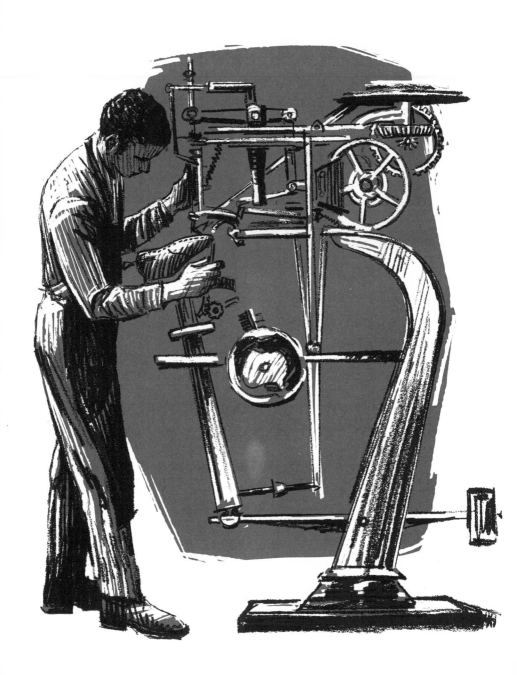

For years, he worked night after night. At last, he built a machine that could put together a whole shoe by itself. It could do this in one minute. Now, instead of turning out sixty pairs of shoes in a day, the men in the shop turned out a thousand pairs. Jan had done "the impossible."

Matzeliger sold his machine for a few thousand dollars. The company that bought it made millions on it. Even today, the United Shoe Machinery Company uses the same kind of machine that Jan built.

The many, many nights of hard work were too much for Jan. Shortly after his machine was finished, his health began to fail. A few years later, at the early age of thirty-seven, he died. The little money he made on his invention came too late to save his health.

Shoes made by machine cost half as much as those made by hand. We can thank Matzeliger for the low price of shoes today.

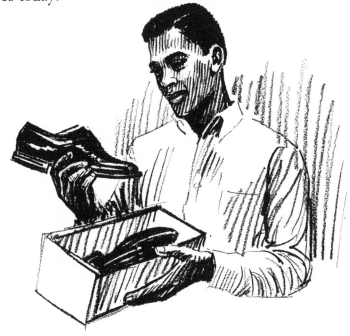

9

Pass to Freedom...

FREDERICK DOUGLASS

Most boys are always hungry. Fred was hungry, but not for food. He was hungry to learn. He wanted to read.

But Fred was a slave. And as a slave he knew it would be hard to feed this hunger. The law did not let a master teach a slave to read.

However, Fred's mistress was kind to him. Along with her own son, she taught him to read. Fred loved his lessons.

Then, one day, in the middle of the afternoon, the master came home. He saw the slave boy learning to read. He became very angry. "Reading will spoil any slave!" he shouted. Poor Fred. There were no more lessons.

But this made him more hungry to learn. He found an old spelling book in the trash one day. Was he happy! "Now," he thought, "if I can only find someone to help me." He knew that some of the white schoolboys would rather eat than read. Since Fred could not go to school, he thought of a plan. He would feed their stomachs if they would feed his brain. To do this, he took cookies from his master's kitchen and gave them to the white boys. They were always hungry, and the cookies tasted good. They taught him what they had learned at school each day.

Now, he could put letters together and make words. Later, he worked on the docks. He studied the words on boxes and barrels that came from ships. He took pieces of wood from the barrels. Then he wrote these words on wooden boards each day. Soon he could read very well.

As a young man he felt a new hunger. He wanted to be free. He did not want to be a slave. So he thought up a bold plan. He asked a Negro sailor to lend him his sailor suit and his papers. There was an eagle, an American eagle, on the papers. This suit and these papers were Fred's pass to freedom.

The next day, he waited behind the station for the train. It came puffing in. As it began to pull out, Fred ran and jumped onto the end car. It was lucky for him that the conductor did not look closely at his papers. So Fred escaped from his master.

After a restless journey by train and steamboat, he reached New York. Now that he was free, he kept working to free all slaves. He read the writings of famous men. He learned to write well and to speak well. Many people came to listen to him. He told them of the hard life of a slave. He told them what he had done to escape. The things he talked about and wrote about were really true.

Books and newspapers carried his stories. This made the slave masters very angry. To escape with his life he had to run away to England. He stayed there for two years. His speeches there turned many people against slavery. They tried to get him to live there in freedom. But Fred wanted to return to America and help his people. This he did.

Frederick Douglass spent hours talking with President Abraham Lincoln. He told him how important it was to stop slavery. What he said helped Lincoln to decide to free the slaves.

Frederick Douglass was one of the greatest orators in our country's history. An orator is a fine speaker. He spoke and worked for freedom for all. He was a leader. The people who loved him have built a statue to honor his memory.

10

No Way but Down...

MATTHEW HENSON

Just about the coldest place on earth is the North Pole. Nothing is farther north than that. Of course, there's no pole there, not even land — only the thick ice that covers the Arctic Ocean. But Commander Peary wanted to plant the American flag there.

He knew he could not do this alone. He needed others

to do many things. And he needed a helper who knew what to do. This helper must make friends with the Eskimos. They must be the guides. The helper must be able to stand the terrible cold. It sometimes froze a man's feet and hands. A man could lose toes and fingers if they were frozen. And the helper must be able to take care of Eskimo dogs and sleds. What man could do all this?

There was one man who had traveled with Commander Peary before on many of his trips. This man was Matthew Henson, a Negro from Maryland. The Eskimos liked Henson, for he spoke their language. He had shown that he could stand the cold of the far north. So Peary asked Henson to go with him to the North Pole.

On a July morning in 1908, Commander Peary and his party set out from New York for the North Pole. They sailed by ship as far north as they could go. After that, they traveled over the ice on sleds pulled by dogs.

Henson and one or two Eskimo guides would go ahead of the rest for a few miles. There they would set up camp. This meant cutting a trail with an ice ax. It meant hiding food in an ice house where others could find it. Things would be ready when the rest of the party reached the new camp. Every few days, Henson would make another trip and set up another camp. Nearer and nearer they came to the North Pole.

At last they reached the North Pole. Peary's compass told them they were there. No matter which way they turned, they would be going south. On April 6, 1909, Peary and Henson planted the American flag, the first to fly at the top of the world. Henson and Peary were the only Americans at the North Pole.

The Present

These are stories of men and women of today. We see them in person. We learn about them in the news. Some speak. Some sing. Some run. Some act. They add to the stories of what Negroes have done in the past. They are part of the story of twentieth-century America.

A. Philip Randolph

Ralph Bunche

Marian Anderson

Thurgood Marshall

Benjamin O. Davis, Jr.

Jackie Robinson

Sidney Poitier

Althea Gibson

Martin Luther King, Jr.

Willie Mays

11

Working Man's Hero...
A. PHILIP RANDOLPH

"Don't you dare let me catch you riding on a street-car in this town!" Philip's mother repeated this to him over and over. Her voice became soft. She said to him, "It is better to walk."

While her two boys were young, Mrs. Randolph began to prepare them to face life. She taught them to hate

segregation. This means keeping races of people apart. She did not want them to ride in the back of the car. Philip never forgot this. He walked many a block in his Florida home town.

Reverend Randolph, Philip's father, was a traveling preacher. He served in two or three country churches. A favorite pastime of Philip's was reading his father's sermons. He enjoyed the plays of William Shakespeare. Before long, he had read all the books in his father's library.

After high school, he went to New York. He was eager to go to college. During the day he worked at many jobs. Sometimes he was an elevator boy. At other times he was a bus boy or waiter. At night he went to the College of the City of New York.

On every job he saw the workers badly treated. Most of them were not paid enough. He tried to get them together to talk about it. For this, he was fired as a trouble-maker.

Philip knew that his fellow workers needed help. He saw that each man was afraid of his boss. No worker would speak out, for fear of losing his job. Philip thought that the men should work together. The bosses could not fire them all. He decided to tell them this.

A few days later, the police carried him off to jail. He had made a speech to some of the workers. He had told them how important it was to work together. They must *organize*. The bosses didn't like this. They were afraid the men would ask for higher pay.

People heard of this man who was not afraid to speak out. The Negro railroad workers needed help. Someone must lead them in their fight for better pay. Randolph became their leader.

They called themselves the Brotherhood of Sleeping Car Porters. He won for them certain rights. They could count on an exact amount of money each week. This was wonderful news! They no longer had to fear that passengers would not tip them well. Until this time, they had lived on tips alone.

This Brotherhood was the first Negro organization, or group, to join the American Federation of Labor. Sometimes this name is written *A. F. L.* This is our largest labor union, or trade group. A. Philip Randolph took the Brotherhood into the A. F. L. He knew this would make the bosses listen.

Next, Mr. Randolph went to Washington. He visited President Franklin Roosevelt in the White House. He talked with him about his own work with the labor unions. Then he asked for this great man's help. He said that Negroes needing jobs were not being hired. The President promised to help him.

Within a short time, Roosevelt kept his word. An order went out across the nation. It said that companies doing government work must hire men of all colors.

Young Mr. Randolph had spoken out. In time, his men lost their fears. Other leaders spoke out too. Now a worker is paid for what he does. And many jobs are open to men of all colors.

Today, when A. Philip Randolph speaks, thousands of people listen. He has been given many honors. He is one of our nation's greatest labor leaders.

12

Pathfinder for Peace...
RALPH BUNCHE

Did you ever ride a trolley car? There wasn't a bus in use on the streets in 1918. Most of the people rode the trolley cars.

42

The boy running beside this trolley car is Ralph Bunche. He did this because of his great love for his mother. She loved music, and Ralph went with her to band concerts. But they were poor and had car fare for only one. So Ralph let his mother ride inside the car. He ran along beside it.

Ralph was about sixteen years old when his mother and father died. He went to Los Angeles and lived with his grandmother. She was a tiny lady and she was very poor. Ralph said that she was the strongest woman he had ever known. He called her Nana. She told him one thing that he never forgot. It was this: "Your color has nothing to do with your worth. You can be as good as anyone."

One day, Ralph came to Nana and told her that he was going to stop school. He was going to work. She stood very still. Then she quietly answered him in five words: "You are going to college." Ralph knew then that he could not stop school.

To stay in school he had to work at many kinds of jobs. He carried newspapers. He worked as a pig boy (carried lead bricks in a print shop). He worked long hours in a bakery. And with all these jobs, he made high marks in school. After his four years in high school, he finished at the head of his class.

Now Ralph was ready to go to college. But where was the money to come from? He got an idea. He and a friend bought a Model T Ford for $25.

They cleaned lunch rooms and shops for people. You should have seen that Ford! Pails, mops, and brooms stuck out on the sides. They went honking and clanging through the streets of Los Angeles. They made enough money to keep them in college.

At the same time, Ralph was becoming a sports champion. He won three small gold basketballs. These pieces of jewelry he wore proudly, pinned to his sweater. He was star player on the team. This was not easy, for Ralph was not tall.

Graduation time came at the University of California at Los Angeles. Ralph Bunche had earned the highest honors. For his fine work he was given a fellowship. This is money for more study at a university. It is not easy to win a fellowship. But Ralph did it.

When he finished, he was known as *Dr.* Bunche. He is not the kind of doctor who cures sick people. He is a doctor of governments. He knows how countries are run, all over the world.

One day a few years later, Dr. Bunche received an important message. He was asked to work at the United Nations. This group tries to help nations keep peace. He took the job. He became best-known when he was good enough to settle a quarrel between Israel and Jordan. For

this he was given the Nobel Peace Prize. Every year this prize is given to the one person in the world who has done the most for peace.

The President of the United States called Dr. Bunche to Washington to be Assistant Secretary of State for the nation. But Dr. Bunche wanted to work in a different kind of job. He chose to help people all over the world. He became head of a part of the United Nations. This group cares for lands and peoples not yet free. This is a very big job.

Thus, study and hard work showed him that Nana's words were true: *Your color has nothing to do with your worth.*

13

World in Her Hands...
MARIAN ANDERSON

When Marian and her father left the pawn shop that day, she was carrying a long box. Inside that box was a violin that Marian had wanted for a long time. Her father had just paid $3.45 for it. But now there was no money for lessons. Marian would have to pick out her own tunes. She loved music so much that this did not matter.

One afternoon about two years later, neighbors crowded around the Andersons' front door. They had come to welcome a piano. Moving men were lifting it up the two white front steps. The neighbors were all very proud. It was the first piano on their street.

Marian sang in the church choir. No voice was like hers. Few women could reach her high notes. Few men could reach her low notes. Sometimes she was called upon to sing the men's parts. She was called "Marian Anderson, Baby Contralto." A contralto can sing the lowest notes for a woman's voice. With such a voice, her mother knew that she needed training. So Mrs. Anderson saved every penny that she could.

After Marian's first year in high school, her mother decided to send her to a music school in their own city, Philadelphia. Marian went into the office of the school carrying her mother's savings to pay for the lessons. She waited for quite a while. Finally, a woman came out and said, "Oh, you still here? Well, we don't take colored."

Back to her own high school went Marian. Luckily for her, she had friends among her teachers. One of them knew a very famous singing teacher. This man agreed to listen to her sing. When he heard her, he knew that she had something. Yes, he would give her lessons, he said, but that would cost money. This time, her friends in the church came to her and told her that somehow they would get the money for the lessons.

Marian worked hard for the next few years. She studied, she practiced, and at last, she sang.

Then the day came when her teacher asked her to enter a contest in New York. This meant that Marian would try out her voice against three hundred other singers. Marian came out first.

Marian would one day sing around the world. She must know the languages of the world. The next few years she spent in Europe. She learned French, German, and Italian.

She felt lonely away from home. She used every minute for her work. This kept her from missing her family too much.

Her first big concert (singing before a group of people) was given in Paris, France. Her proud mother sat there and wiped away tears of joy. Marian's voice had magic for her audience (people who listened). When she finished,

they jumped to their feet. Their clapping sounded like thunder. Their voices roared their delight.

Marian Anderson returned to America. She was the world's greatest contralto. But she had not yet sung for an American audience. She was prepared to do this even though she was afraid. Would an American audience like a Negro on the concert stage?

The American audiences she feared did just what the Paris audiences had done. They took her to their hearts. A musician known around the world, Arturo Toscanini (Ar-TUR-o Tos-ca-NI-ni), wrote about her. He said, "A voice like hers comes once in a hundred years."

Many other honors have come to her. Marian Anderson was the first Negro to sing at the Metropolitan Opera. She was asked by the President of the United States to sit at the United Nations for the United States government.

Many great artists have painted her picture. She has sung before kings and queens and rulers all over the world.

Her own city, Philadelphia, presented her with a $10,000 gift for her work. She gave it all to help young people who want to study music. This is called the Marian Anderson Award. It is given without thought of race.

In 1965, Marian Anderson decided it was time to stop singing. She left the stage. Luckily for us, she has made many records. We can still hear her sing "The Whole World in His Hands." And we can still hear her sing many other songs in many different languages. Marian Anderson is one of the greatest singers America has known.

14

Up from the Basement...

THURGOOD MARSHALL

No boy knew his school basement better than Thurgood. He spent many, many days there, alone. And why in the basement? That was the way his principal punished him for breaking rules. He could not come up until he had learned a part of the United States Constitution by heart.

By the time he finished school, Thurgood knew the whole Constitution (the laws of our country).

Just a little education was not enough for him. After high school, he went to Lincoln University. He then tried to get into the University of Maryland. But he could not get in, because he was a Negro. Instead, he finished law school at Howard University, with honors. To be a lawyer he needed an office. To fix it up his mother gave him the rug from her living room floor. He opened the office — and he waited for months. Almost no one came.

He went on in this way for a year or two. Then, one day, an angry young student came into his office. He told Marshall that the University of Maryland would not let him enter, because he was a Negro. This was the same school that had kept out Thurgood. The young lawyer was happy to take the case. He took it to the Maryland court. He won the case. This changed his life. The leaders of the N. A. A. C. P. heard of him. Immediately, Thurgood Marshall was hired as their lawyer.

Mr. Marshall leaped into fame after many years of hard work. In 1954, he won a Supreme Court decision. This was a ruling by the highest court in the land. This ruling was on school desegregation. School desegregation means the mixing of races in schools. Mr. Marshall argued for desegregation. He explained the case to the Supreme Court. The nine judges listened to him carefully. They decided he was right. He won the case.

Another step upward came to him when President Kennedy named him to be a federal judge. This meant that he would serve in a court of the United States.

Then, President Johnson asked him to be Solicitor General of the United States. Mr. Marshall became one of the top law officers of the land. As Solicitor General, he took charge of the cases brought before the Supreme Court. He spoke before the court for the United States.

In 1967, Mr. Marshall reached the top. President Johnson named him to the Supreme Court. Nine judges make up this court. This is the highest court in the land. What these men decide becomes law in the United States. Thurgood Marshall is the first Negro ever to serve on this court.

Supreme Court Justice Marshall must be saying "Thank you" a million times to his school principal. He made him learn the United States Constitution. Little did that principal know that he was training Thurgood Marshall for the Supreme Court of the United States.

15

Hero at West Point...
BENJAMIN O. DAVIS, JR.

I was proud and very happy the morning that I arrived at West Point. The test that I had taken to enter was hard, but I had passed it. I thought to myself, "Benjamin O. Davis, Jr., you've made it."

Only three Negroes before me had graduated from the United States Military Academy. This is the United States

training school for Army officers. Perhaps it was because of this that I had made up my mind that I would not fail. I went about eagerly making friends with the other plebes (new students). I loved every minute of it!

Then something happened. I saw and heard whispering. No one spoke to me. If I walked up to a group that were talking, they became silent.

I thought to myself, "Why are they doing this to me? They were all so friendly at the beginning. I feel so alone! Can it be because I am the only Negro here?"

I could feel something inside me become hard. I stood up tall and said to myself, "I'll not let them think I need them for my happiness. Too many people are counting on me. I'll stick it out. I can take whatever they dish out to me." For months, this queer game went on.

Toward the end of the year, a note came to me asking that I come to a meeting of the plebes. Many plebes had dropped out during the year. I decided to go just to see what would happen.

Something did happen. Suddenly, I found myself in the middle of a crowd. They shook and shook my hand until my arm was weak.

I learned that this had been their way of testing me. They called this *hazing*. Every plebe goes through some kind of hazing. Someone told me later that I had passed the hardest test of any boy at West Point.

Four years later, I was graduated as a second lieutenant in the United States Army. After a year's work with the Army, I became a first lieutenant. Within a few years, I went from captain to major to lieutenant colonel. I was training Negro troops only.

About this time, our government was looking for Negroes to serve in the Air Force. I wanted to be a flyer, so I trained for a year. I became an aviator. My wings, the silver sign of the flyer, were pinned to my coat.

I finished my training just in time to serve in World War II. I was named commander (man in charge) of the 99th Pursuit (chasing) Squadron (part of a group). Their

acts of bravery made history. It was their job to protect the U.S. bombers from enemy fighters. So bold were they that their color was forgotten. Soon, Negro bombardiers (men who drop the bombs), navigators (men who guide the planes), and flight engineers were part of the U.S. Air Force.

My proudest moment came after World War II. I was made a brigadier general. My father, Benjamin O. Davis, Sr., was our country's first Negro general. My family has served its country well.

Today, I command the 13th American Air Force in the Philippines. On my door you will find this sign:

LIEUTENANT GENERAL B. O. DAVIS, JR.

16

One in Nine...

JACKIE ROBINSON

"Play ball!"

This was the signal to start the first big game of the new season. The nine players came running out onto the playing field. The noisy crowd was suddenly very quiet. Every eye followed *one* player. He was Jackie Robinson.

Never before had a Negro played in the big leagues. Was he as good as the newspapers had said he was? He was even better.

Ask the thousands of excited fans how good he was. They will tell you that in his first game Jackie hit a three-run homer and three singles. He batted in four runs and stole two bases. This was the speed the Dodgers needed.

Jackie had been a schoolboy in California. It had been hard for his mother to care for five small children alone. His father had died when Jackie was small. Sometimes a five-cent bag of peanuts was his lunch. He said that he ate the nuts because he liked the taste and that he ate the shells because they helped fill him up.

BASKETBALL

FOOTBALL

BASEBALL

TRACK

All through his high school and college days he was
a sports star. Basketball, football, baseball, track; he was

champ in them all. Win or lose, he always played hard, and he was always fair.

Later, he played shortstop for a small-time Negro baseball team. With the pay from this job, he was able to take care of his mother.

One day, a strange man came to visit him. He told Jackie that he was a baseball scout. His job was to find good players. He wanted Jackie to go to New York. This was his chance to try out for the Brooklyn Dodgers.

"A big-league team," thought Jackie. He laughed in the man's face. No Negro had ever played in the big leagues. The Dodger team was really big-time.

He promised to go, but he didn't. He felt that they would never let a Negro play in the big leagues.

The scout returned after a few weeks and asked him again. This time, Jackie did go to New York. He was signed up right away. This made history. For the first time, a Negro was to play in big-league baseball.

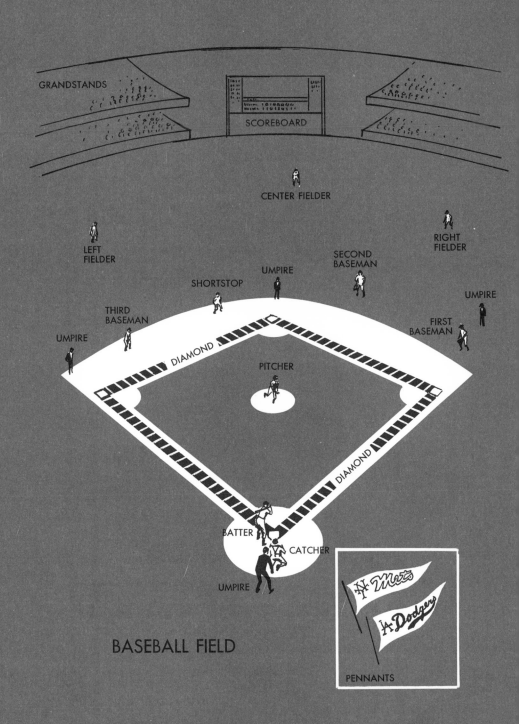

GRANDSTANDS

SCOREBOARD

CENTER FIELDER

LEFT
FIELDER

RIGHT
FIELDER

UMPIRE

SECOND
BASEMAN

SHORTSTOP

UMPIRE

THIRD
BASEMAN

FIRST
BASEMAN

UMPIRE

DIAMOND

PITCHER

DIAMOND

BATTER

CATCHER

UMPIRE

BASEBALL FIELD

PENNANTS

People said, "The teams will not play with him. The fans will not come to the games. There will be race riots."

They were wrong. Most players treated him fairly. Crowds came — just to see *him* play. There were no race riots. Newspapers printed more about him than about any other player.

The Dodgers won the National League Pennant that year. This is the flag that goes to the best team in its league. Jackie put excitement into the game for players and fans.

After his second year, he was named the league's Most Valuable Player. He played for twelve years. Then he left baseball. He became vice president of Chock Full O' Nuts. This is a chain of eating places.

Jackie can be heard on radio or seen on television. People want to know his ideas on things. He has been an aide to the Governor of New York State.

He played with skill, speed, and fine teamwork. These won for him a place in baseball's Hall of Fame. A player can receive no higher honor.

17

The Do-It-Yourself Actor...
SIDNEY POITIER

The stars looked down on Sidney Poitier (POI-ti-er). He was lying on a Broadway rooftop. He pulled his coat close around him to keep warm.

He could not sleep. He looked back at the stars and thought, "What am I doing up here?" Sidney knew the

answer. He shook with cold and said aloud, "I have no place to go." He wondered if he should have left the warm Florida sunshine — for this.

He was just sixteen, and he had left his brother's home in Florida because he saw no chance of becoming an actor there. Now acting was what Sidney wanted most to do. So with $1.50 in his pocket he ran away and hitchhiked to New York.

There was just about no job that he did not try. He was dishwasher, truck driver, ditch digger, parking lot man, waiter, and bus boy.

One day, Sidney read an ad in a New York paper: "Wanted—Actors—American Negro Theater!" This was his

chance. But when he tried out for the part, he was told
that his words were not spoken clearly enough.

He wanted to be an actor. The do-it-yourself way was
his only way. He began to teach himself.

First, he bought a radio for $14. And for six months
he listened to the best speakers on the air. He practiced
speaking as they did. He carried a dictionary in his pocket.
He spent hours, every day, learning the words that would
help him master the English language.

When he was sure that he was ready, he went back
to the American Negro Theater. This time, he got a job.

He became an understudy. This meant that he would take the parts of actors who were ill. Sidney was happy. He was on his way.

His way led him from understudy to actor. He played small parts in three Broadway shows. Then he got bigger parts to play. At last, Sidney Poitier saw his name in lights.

This was his dream come true. He was now a working actor. He was being paid for doing what he wanted most to do. In time, he was able to build a home for his parents.

Sidney Poitier and Ruby Dee in A Raisin in the Sun

Sidney Poitier and Mildred Smith
in No Way Out

Sidney Poitier
and Tony Curtis
in The Defiant O...

Sidney Poitier and Lilia Skala
in Lilies of the Field

70

The next stop on his way was Hollywood. Sidney was over six feet tall and very handsome. It was not long before he became the favorite hero of thousands of movie fans.

His first film was *No Way Out*. In it Sidney played the part of a doctor. His next picture, *The Defiant Ones*, made him a star. In this picture, he neither sang nor danced. His acting alone proved he was a star.

Sidney Poitier reached the top in 1964. He won movieland's highest prize, the Oscar. This is a golden statue given each year by Hollywood to the man it chooses as the best actor. Sidney Poitier was named as the best actor of that year for his role (part) in *Lilies of the Field*. He was the first Negro to receive this honor.

There was no magic at work for Sidney Poitier. He reached the top only because he was willing to spend long, long hours at hard, hard work.

Sidney Poitier Receives the Oscar

18

Girl with a Racket...

ALTHEA GIBSON

Hundreds of kids were heading for one block in Harlem. It was a *P A L* (Police Athletic League) play street. It was marked off with white lines. This meant that during the day it was closed to cars and trucks. But today was a special day, very special. Everybody was going to watch the finals in the summer Paddle Tennis Games.

Althea Gibson was the Paddle Tennis winner for this block. Today, she must face the winners from all the other blocks. The play-off would decide the Harlem Paddle Tennis Championship.

Althea was tops. She could hit a ball sharply and land it right where she wanted to. How excited the kids were when they saw her leap up or spin around to return a ball! Before long, the shouts and squeals of her fans told that Althea was the winner. The Paddle Tennis Medal for Harlem was hers.

Her family never had too much money. Althea's father was a cotton farmer. Hoping to give them a better life, he had brought his family to New York from South Carolina. But things were pretty hard for him here. Althea was on her own a lot. She soon got used to the gangs in the streets. These boys stole money wherever they could. When she saw one of them trying to rob her uncle, she fought him to a draw. She was very strong, and she was not afraid.

One dream stayed with her always: "I want to be somebody." She did not know it, but she took her first step toward being somebody when she won that medal in a Harlem street. Now she was in line to try out for the championship of all Manhattan. This play-off would be held in the park. She played and won. At the age of twelve, Althea Gibson, a Negro girl from Harlem, won the Manhattan Trophy for Park Paddle Tennis.

Althea stayed in school until she finished high school. But her big interest was ball games. A family friend saw her love of sports. He bought her a real tennis racket. He taught her good manners on a tennis court. He taught her real sportsmanship by saying to her again and again, "Don't get mad, Althea." He dressed her in real tennis clothes. Then, she met some of the top tennis players. Practicing tennis now became all-important to her.

She was soon ready to play against the best. But Althea was a Negro. She did not know how good she was. No Negro had been allowed to play in the National Championship games. Then, one day, an invitation came asking her to enter the Women's National Tennis Championship games at Forest Hills, New York.

On the first day, rain stopped the game. To Althea, this was a bad sign. She spent most of that night with no sleep. She told herself that she'd never make it. The next day she lost the game.

She was good—Althea knew that—but not good enough. So she decided to go to college. She finished and became a gym teacher. During all this time, she kept working on her tennis, trying to play a better game.

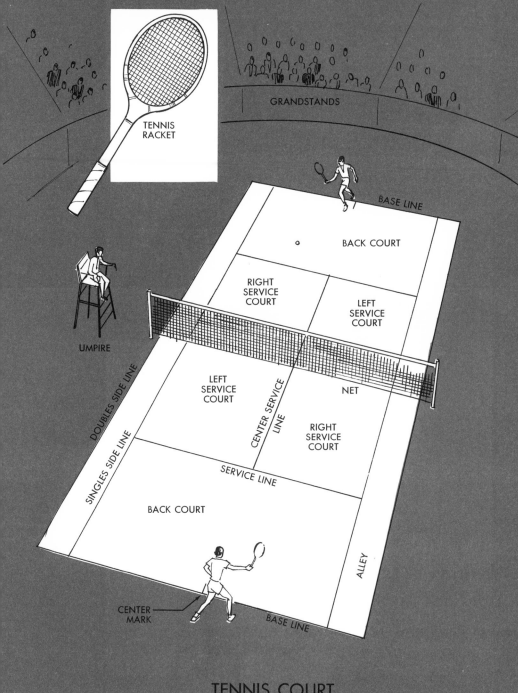

TENNIS RACKET

GRANDSTANDS

BASE LINE

BACK COURT

RIGHT SERVICE COURT

LEFT SERVICE COURT

UMPIRE

DOUBLES SIDE LINE

SINGLES SIDE LINE

LEFT SERVICE COURT

CENTER SERVICE LINE

NET

RIGHT SERVICE COURT

SERVICE LINE

BACK COURT

ALLEY

CENTER MARK

BASE LINE

TENNIS COURT

"Perhaps now," she thought, "I am ready to make another try at the tennis championship." First, she went to England. There, she won the Wimbledon matches. That meant that she was the best tennis player in England. She was greeted by the Queen.

There was now just one more prize that Althea had to win. So back to New York she came — to Forest Hills. It was National Championship time again. She played against the same woman who had beaten her before. This time, Althea won. She was now tennis champion of the world. The dream had come true. *She was now somebody.* She was the greatest woman tennis player in the world.

Later, she wrote the story of her life. She called it — yes, you've guessed it — *I ALWAYS WANTED TO BE SOMEBODY.*

19

A Chance to Speak...
MARTIN LUTHER KING, JR.

Shouts of joy rang out. The State of Georgia had chosen its contest winner. He was riding a bus with a happy group of junior high school boys and girls. Martin Luther King had won the second prize in the speaking contest that the state held each year.

Onto the bus came a group of white people. The stu-

dents were ordered to give up their seats to them. Then
and there, Martin Luther King made up his mind not to
get mad — but *to do something*.

By the time he got to college, he had decided to become
a minister. Then, he thought, he would have a chance to
speak to many people. He studied famous people like
Harriet Tubman and Frederick Douglass. He read about
the great Indian leader Gandhi. This great man believed
that he could free his people without guns or fighting.
Martin Luther King thought and thought. He made up
his mind to follow Gandhi's way to free his own people.

Twenty years later, Negroes were still being told to give up their seats in buses in the South. But on an evening in 1955, one Negro lady in Montgomery would not obey. She would not give up her seat. She was put in jail.

"Now," thought the well-trained minister and leader Dr. Martin Luther King, "I have my chance to speak. I shall speak to my people and lead them to freedom. This I will do without fighting and without guns."

He said to them, "No Negro must ride the buses for *any* reason."

They obeyed him. They used wagons, cars, and taxis. Some walked. But they never rode a bus. This was called a *boycott*.

After almost a year with no Negro riders, the bus line

lost lots of money. It had to go out of business. The Negroes won — without fighting and without guns. They got the right to sit wherever they wished on the buses.

This was only the first of the battles that Dr. King won when he got his "chance to speak." This true story goes down in history as the Montgomery Bus Boycott.

Dr. King is known the world over as a peaceful fighter. He tries to get people's rights — not with guns, but with words.

He was given the Nobel Peace Prize in 1964. Every year, this honor may be won. It is given to the one person in the world who has worked most for peace.

With this honor goes a gift of $35,000. Dr. King did not keep a penny for himself. He gave it all for his work.

20

"Say-Hey"...

WILLIE MAYS

Willie Mays started to run not too many months after he was born. He couldn't wait to walk.

His grandfather was a baseball player. When Willie could crawl, Grandfather would roll a ball to him. If he could not stop it, Willie would somehow get to his feet

and run after the ball. Then, back to his grandfather he would crawl with the ball. Both of them loved this game.

Aunt Sarah took care of Willie. He loved her dearly all her life. She felt that a Negro had no chance in baseball. So she asked Grandfather to stop talking and teaching baseball to Willie. But Grandfather did not agree. Thus, under Grandfather's watchful eyes, Willie ran and ran and grew and grew.

When he finished high school in Alabama, Willie knew what he wanted to be. He said, "I do not want to be a

laundry presser." This is what he had learned in Fairfield Vocational School.

"I do not want to work in a mill as my father did. I want to be a baseball player."

This made Aunt Sarah worry.

He started as a fielder with the Birmingham Barons, a Negro team. This gave Willie a good start.

But this was not for long. Soon, scouts from the New York Giants visited the team. Before he knew it, Willie was on the train for Minnesota. And whom do you think he met before his first game there? He met the famous Leo Durocher.

"Hi ya, Skip," said Willie.

"Hi ya, Willie," answered Leo. "I hear you're quite a boy!"

In his first game, Willie proved just that. He really put on a show. He singled; he tripled; he hit a home run. Later, he caught a long fly ball. He threw the ball to home plate in time to catch a runner.

"He's the greatest!" cried Durocher. "We've got to have him."

And so Willie became one of the New York Giants (now the San Francisco Giants). Soon he was called the most exciting player in baseball.

His pals loved to tease him after the games. When he tried to tell them about one of his fast plays on the field, they would all start shouting. To quiet them down, he'd call, "Say!" They would all yell louder. Then he would shout back, "Hey!" trying to make them listen to him. Then, all together, they'd call him "Say-Hey Willie!"

He was twice voted the Most Valuable Player of the National League. Several times he was named batting champ of the league. He has never missed playing in an All-Star game.

"He can beat any player four ways," said one newspaper, "arms, legs, gloves, and bat."

Today, Willie Mays, the "Say-Hey Kid," is one of the highest-paid baseball players of all time. He is certainly the greatest player on his team. He is admired both as a player and as a man.

A MATCHING GAME

Now that you have finished the book, here is a game to play. Find the letter that belongs with each number below.

1. Crispus Attucks
2. Marian Anderson
3. Benjamin Banneker
4. Henry Box Brown
5. Ralph Bunche

6. Benjamin O. Davis, Jr.

7. Frederick Douglass
8. Althea Gibson
9. Matthew Henson

10. Martin Luther King, Jr.
11. Thurgood Marshall
12. Jan Matzeliger
13. Willie Mays
14. A. Philip Randolph
15. Jackie Robinson
16. Peter Salem

17. Harriet Tubman

18. Underground Railroad

19. Sidney Poitier

20. Constitution

a. singer
b. slave — escaped in a box
c. West Point soldier
d. tennis star
e. died in the Boston Massacre
f. explorer at the North Pole
g. laws of our country
h. led a bus boycott
i. invented a labor-saving machine
j. Dodgers' infielder
k. secret escape for slaves
l. wrote an almanac
m. labor leader
n. Underground general
o. actor
p. slave — escaped dressed as a sailor
q. leader in the United Nations
r. Justice of the Supreme Court
s. soldier at the Battle of Bunker Hill
t. Giants' outfielder

About
the
Stories

1

What the Bells Told . . .

CRISPUS ATTUCKS

DO YOU KNOW

1. why Crispus ran away?
2. why he returned after twenty years?

LET'S LOOK AT WORDS.

1. Find three words in the story having the *e* sound spelled in each of these three ways. (One of each is given for you.)

e	ee	ea
he	free	each

2. Some words have more than one meaning. Find the meanings that these words have in the story:

arms	ring	clubs
parts of the body	jewelry	sticks
weapons	noise of a bell	groups of people

CAN YOU

1. give the Americans and the Redcoats their *own* weapons? There were clubs, guns, fists, and bayonets.
2. tell three things about the first American to die for his country's freedom?
    a. his name
    b. the battle in which he died
    c. the city where the battle took place

WHAT DO YOU THINK?

Should Crispus Attucks, the slave, have returned to fight for the freedom of all Americans? Why or why not?

2

School in the Sky ...

BENJAMIN BANNEKER

DO YOU KNOW

four things Benjamin did that showed he had a fine brain?

LET'S LOOK AT WORDS.

Word Building

1. Make three words, each ending in *y*.
    - *a.* Begin each with *sl, sk,* or *dr*.
    - *b.* Use only three letters.
    - *c.* Match your word meanings with:
      clever, what Ben gazed at, not wet

2. Make three words, each ending with *ll*.
    - *a.* Begin words with *b, f,* or *m*.
    - *b.* Use only four letters.
    - *c.* Match your word meanings with:
      a bird's beak, to make full, where the wheat was ground

3. Make three words, each ending with *eel*.
    - *a.* Begin words with *kn, wh,* or *st*.
    - *b.* Use five letters.
    - *c.* Match your word meanings with:

to get down on your knees, a metal, what was
spinning at the mill
4. Make three words, each ending in *ound*.
    a. Begin each with *r*, *gr*, or *s*.
    b. Use five or six letters.
    c. Match your word meanings with:
       what the wheels did to the wheat, a noise,
       shaped like a circle

CAN YOU

match the items in List A with the items in List B?

A	**B**
astronomer	friend
city planner	skies
Ellicott	almanac
clock	Washington, D.C.
writer	knife

WHAT DO YOU THINK?

Can you suggest a better title for this story?

3

A Shot from the Hill . . .

PETER SALEM

DO YOU KNOW
1. why
    a. the Minutemen were ready to fight?

    b. Peter Salem, the slave, fought with them?

2. how to finish *a*, *b*, and *c*? Pick two of the four numbers for each.

    a. The Minutemen

1. were afraid	3. had little training
2. were angry	4. had good guns

    b. Peter Salem

1. ran away	3. hated the Minutemen
2. wanted to be free	4. shot Major Pitcairn

    c. The Redcoats

1. had fine guns	3. wore blue coats
2. shot Major Pitcairn	4. made the Americans angry

LET'S LOOK AT WORDS.

Read the following sentences. Each underlined word has two meanings. Find the correct meaning below for each underlined word.

    a. The soldiers had to return <u>rounds</u> of shots.

        1. circles   2. number of shots

    b. They hid their <u>arms</u> behind the wall.

        1. parts of the body   2. guns

    c. The soldiers sat near the <u>fire</u>.

        1. flames   2. shoot

    d. The <u>stone</u> wall hid them from the enemy.

        1. rock   2. jewel

CAN YOU

line up these words for the

<u>AMERICANS</u>   and the   <u>BRITISH?</u>

Redcoats, sticks and stones, Peter Salem, a lot of training, fine guns, wall of earth and stones, little training, best soldiers, Minutemen, Major Pitcairn, old muskets

(Put each word under the right heading.)

WHAT DO YOU THINK?

The Minutemen were braver than the Redcoats. Do you agree?

4

Escape . . .

THE UNDERGROUND RAILROAD

DO YOU KNOW

1. which five letters below refer to parts of the Underground Railroad?

Words from the Story

a. carts and wagons   *f.* kind people

b. masters   *g.* jails

c. runaway slaves   *h.* engines

d. Quakers   *i.* railroad trains

e. slave-catchers   *j.* secret

2. that the sentences below are five Steps to Freedom? Arrange them in the right order.

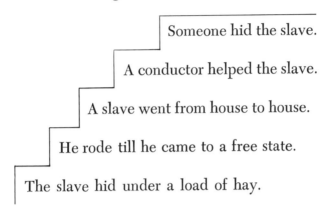

Someone hid the slave.

A conductor helped the slave.

A slave went from house to house.

He rode till he came to a free state.

The slave hid under a load of hay.

LET'S LOOK AT WORDS.

Here are four compound words (two words put together to make one word) from the story:

underground   runaway   railroad   sometimes

For each word choose its meaning in *this* story.

escaped   **secret**

now and then   **a way of escape**

CAN YOU

1. name three trains on the Underground Railroad?
2. tell what the railroad tracks were on the Underground Railroad?

WHAT DO YOU THINK?

Would you have been a conductor on the Underground Railroad if you had lived at that time? Why?

5

The General Was a Lady...
HARRIET TUBMAN

DO YOU KNOW

1. why Harriet could be called a general?
2. the answers for this number game?
   Pick a number for each of the following:

   _____

   | 19 | $40,000 | 300 |

   _____

   a. reward for Harriet Tubman's capture
   b. number of slaves she led north
   c. number of trips she made north

LET'S LOOK AT WORDS.

There are two meanings for the underlined words in each sentence. Find the right meanings for each.

1. Mother's secret was <u>mine</u>.   hole dug into the ground

2. Coal comes from a <u>mine</u>.   belonging to me

3. Harriet Tubman went <u>back</u> nineteen times.   again

4. I hurt my <u>back</u>.   part of the body

5. You will be <u>safe</u> there.   iron box

6. Money was kept in a <u>safe</u>.   out of danger

7. These are true <u>stories</u>.   floors

8. That station has two <u>stories</u>.   tales

CAN YOU

divide this list into *musts* and *must nots?* (A slave was warned about things he *must* or *must not* do while he was escaping.)

lie still	whisper	lie on the floor
sing	turn back	keep under cover
stand	not be afraid	want to be free

WHAT DO YOU THINK?

Harriet Tubman had good reasons for saying, "There is no turning back." What were they?

6

A Quaker Walks By...

HARRIET TUBMAN

DO YOU KNOW

1. what the surprise was in this story?
2. what words tell us
    a. why Harriet's friend did not answer her knock?
    b. where the slave band hid just before daylight?
    c. who Harriet thought saved her and the slaves?

LET'S LOOK AT WORDS.

1. Picture words help make sentences clear. They help us see pictures of what we read. Find three of them in the story that help us see the following pictures:

a. the kind of face that appeared at the window

b. the kind of grass the band of slaves hid in

c. the way the Quaker talked as he walked by

2. Make six compound words from words in the story.

run	lands
swamp	side
Tub	away
barn	side
in	man
out	yard

3. Put these words in the order of the alphabet.

man	barn
Quaker	farm
friend	horse
talking	food
wagon	path

WHAT DO YOU THINK?

The Quaker in this story did a dangerous thing. Do you agree? Why did he do it?

7

Man in a Box . . .

HENRY BOX BROWN

DO YOU KNOW

which of these newspaper headlines do *not* tell the truth about Brown or McKim—and why not? Give their numbers.

1. Slave Escapes to Freedom

2. Slave Uses Gimlet on Master

3. Slave Goes to Freedom in a Box

4. Slave Leaves Kind Master

5. Train Carries Slave to Freedom by Express

6. Mr. McKim Gives Slave a Longer Name

7. Mr. McKim Is Part of the Underground Railroad

8. Runaway Slave Returned to Master

LET'S LOOK AT WORDS.

Certain words make things clear for us. In the story, find the words that tell the kind of

1. plan Henry made
2. master he left
3. box he stepped into
4. slave Henry was
5. trip he had
6. arms he had when he stood up
7. chains that were broken
8. name Henry would have

CAN YOU

tell which of these eight ideas were Brown's and which were McKim's?

1. to run away
2. to meet the train
3. to go by train
4. to stay alive

5. to take home the box
6. to open the case
7. to go free
8. to give the slave a new name

WHAT DO YOU THINK?

Men were put in jail for helping runaway slaves. What kind of man would take the chance Mr. McKim took?

8

A Shoe a Minute...

JAN MATZELIGER

DO YOU KNOW

about shoemaking BEFORE and AFTER Jan's machine?

1. whole shoe put together by machine
2. hours spent on one shoe
3. sixty pairs made each day
4. parts of shoes put together by hand
5. prices of shoes lower
6. 1000 pairs made each day
7. men worked late
8. men worked slowly

LET'S LOOK AT WORDS.

Here are some twin words. They sound *exactly* alike. Which spelling is correct?

1. We can (buy, by) shoes made (buy, by) that machine.
2. The machine is (so, sew) big that I can't (so, sew) on it.

3. It took (won, one) day to fix that (won, one) shoe.
4. Jan (won, one) (won, one) more friend in the shop.
5. He ate (pairs, pears) with his lunch. Then he finished twenty (pairs, pears) of shoes.
6. (There, Their) machine did not get (there, their) in time.

CAN YOU

go step by step with Jan? Give the order in which these events took place.

> Jan built a machine.
> He died at an early age.
> Jan ran a machine in his father's shop.
> Jan went to Massachusetts.
> A big company bought Jan's machine.
> Shoes were made at less cost.

WHAT DO YOU THINK?

Why was Jan Matzeliger willing to spend so much time on this machine? Why is it important to have the kind of machine that Jan invented?

9

Pass to Freedom ...

FREDERICK DOUGLASS

DO YOU KNOW

1. what Fred did to help his people?

2. what Fred, the boy, was hungry for?
3. what he and Abraham Lincoln talked about?

LET'S LOOK AT WORDS.

Make a compound word (one long word) from two words in the list at the side. In each sentence, use a compound in place of the underlined word.

1. Fred needed <u>a person</u> to help him.
2. His kind mistress helped him every <u>day</u>.
3. The Underground <u>travel</u> was a way to escape.
4. Fred used the <u>secret</u> Railroad when he ran away.
5. He read what he had written, in <u>print</u>.

some	papers
Rail	noon
Under	one
after	ground
news	road

CAN YOU TELL

which words in this list helped Fred?
which words in this list did not help him?

1. mistress
2. the law
3. white boys
4. people in England
5. soldier
6. American eagle
7. his father
8. spelling book
9. sailor
10. master

WHAT DO YOU THINK?

Fred Douglass might have been happier in England. Many people wanted him to stay. Why did he not stay?

10

No Way but Down...

MATTHEW HENSON

DO YOU KNOW

1. three reasons why Peary picked Henson to go with him?
2. these "numbers" answers?
   a. date of leaving for the North Pole?
   b. date of arriving at the North Pole?
   c. number of months they were traveling?

LET'S LOOK AT WORDS.

Play the "Cross-word" game.

Directions: Find two words in the story that have the *same middle letter.* Make a cross of the two words. Here are some examples:

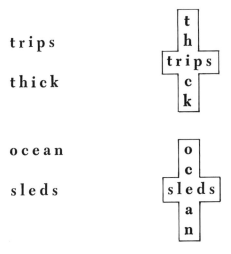

trips

thick

ocean

sleds

How many "Cross-words" can you make from these words?

Eskimos   north   toe   Peary   plant   Americans
thick   party   dog   place   trail   guide

CAN YOU

give the right job to these three?

Henson

Eskimos

Peary

1. pick the men to go on the trip
2. guide the party through the snow
3. make friends with the Eskimos
4. go ahead and make camps
5. plan the trip

WHAT DO YOU THINK?

Why should any man want to go to the North Pole?

11

Working Man's Hero...

A. PHILIP RANDOLPH

LET'S LOOK AT WORDS.

Match these words with their meanings:

1. segregation   group
2. union   keeping races of people apart
3. A. F. L.   work with hands
4. organize   work together
5. labor   American Federation of Labor

DO YOU KNOW

which letters below answer these five questions?

1. Why did Philip walk many blocks in his home town?
2. Why did Philip go to college at night?
3. Why was Philip carried off to jail?
4. Why did the train workers want Mr. Randolph to lead them?
5. Why, do you think, was he called the Working Man's Hero?

    a. He worked during the day.
    b. He helped the working man.
    c. His mother told him not to ride the streetcars.
    d. The workers knew he was not afraid to speak out.
    e. He tried to organize the working men.

CAN YOU

give the order in which these events took place?

Philip read sermons.
He talked with the President of the United States.
Philip was taken to jail.
He led the Brotherhood of Sleeping Car Porters.
He went to New York.

WHAT DO YOU THINK?

1. A. Philip Randolph felt that tips are not enough for people who labor. Do you agree?
2. He should have told his fellow workers to please their bosses. Do you agree?

12

Pathfinder for Peace . . .

RALPH BUNCHE

DO YOU KNOW

1. who was the most important person in Ralph's life?
2. what she told him that proved to be true at the end of the story?
3. what kind of boy Ralph was?

poor boy	lazy boy	kind boy
happy boy	smart boy	obedient boy
mean boy	short boy	sad boy
busy boy	proud boy	thoughtful boy

LET'S LOOK AT WORDS.

1. Find one word in the story that *sounds exactly* like each of these. Don't let spelling fool you.

   fair   ours   piece

2. Play the "L-word" game.
   Directions: Find two words in the story. If one *ends* with the same letter that *begins* the other, you can play the "L-word" game.

   Examples: 1. **p r i n t**

   t i n y

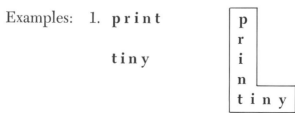

Examples: 2. t r a v e l

lady

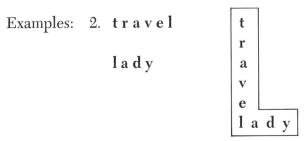

How many "L-words" can you make from these words? Use each word as many times as you wish.

concert	travel	person	magic	nation	clanging
high	players	your	honking	concert	trolley
	Ralph	champ	job	boy	

CAN YOU

1. tell where in the telephone book you would look to find Dr. Bunche's office number?
2. find the sentence that proves Dr. Bunche really cares for people? Look near the end of the story.

WHAT DO YOU THINK?

Should Dr. Bunche have taken the job in Washington? Or should he have stayed at the United Nations? What do you think?

13

World in Her Hands . . .

MARIAN ANDERSON

DO YOU KNOW

1. which of these best tells what the story is about?

a. a girl and her father   *c.* a girl in Europe
b. a girl and her music   *d.* a girl in her church

2. which of these were in Marian's home?

   a. a horn   *c.* a violin
   b. a piano   *d.* a television set

3. which letter best finishes each sentence below?
   Neighbors crowded around the Andersons' front door to
   The name given to Marian Anderson was
   After her Paris concert, the clapping
   Marian started singing in
   The Marian Anderson Award was started for

   a. sounded like thunder   *c.* music students in need
                                        of help
   b. welcome a piano   *d.* Baby Contralto
                     e. her church

LET'S LOOK AT WORDS.

On a paper, number from 1 to 6. After each number write
the whole word about Marian Anderson.

1. Marian Anderson lived in
   P h — — — — — — — — — — a.
2. Her father bought her a v — — — — — —.
3. People who come to listen to a singer are called an
   a u — — — — — — —.
4. She was invited to sit in at the United Nations by the
   — — — s — — — — t.
5. It took many years to train Marian Anderson's
   — — i c e.
6. The money given to help music students is called an
   a — a — —.

CAN YOU

find one word in each line that does *not* go with the first one?

1. **music** — song, piano, steps, violin
2. **family** — Marian, father, mother, lessons
3. **place** — door, Philadelphia, Paris, New York
4. **people** — neighbors, audience, voice, family

WHAT DO YOU THINK?

The City of Philadelphia gave an award of $10,000 to Marian Anderson. She gave it away. What do you think she should have done with it?

14

Up from the Basement . . .
THURGOOD MARSHALL

DO YOU KNOW

1. why Thurgood Marshall must be saying so many thank-you's to the principal in the story?
2. who the first person was to bring a case into his office?
3. whether he won or lost this case?
4. whether these sentences are *true* or *false?*
    a. A little education was enough for Thurgood Marshall.
    b. His mother helped him fix up his office.
    c. President Johnson named Marshall to be a judge.
    d. Marshall is a member of our Supreme Court.

LET'S LOOK AT WORDS.

Find the meaning of these words in the story:
1. Supreme Court.
2. Solicitor General. Explain his job.
3. Federal judge.

CAN YOU NAME

1. two schools in this story?
2. four people in this story?

WHAT DO YOU THINK?

Young Thurgood was punished many times in school. Each time, his principal made him learn more and more of the United States Constitution. Our Constitution is a set of laws. Our country is ruled by it. Thurgood's punishment helped him later in life. Do you agree? Explain.

15

Hero at West Point . . .

BENJAMIN O. DAVIS, JR.

DO YOU KNOW

what Benjamin O. Davis, Jr., was called
1. when he entered West Point?
2. when he left West Point?
3. when he was commander in the Philippines?

LET'S LOOK AT WORDS.

Find the following words in the story. Look for other

words near them that give hints to their meanings. Tell what each word means.

   plebes   hazing   aviator   wings

CAN YOU

remember how Ben felt about West Point?
Choose the words below that fit each title.

First Day   *During Hazing*   *After Leaving*

proud   lonely   hardworking   hurt   strong   happy
cheerful   eager   unhappy   friendly   angry   thankful

WHAT DO YOU THINK?

   When his friends did not speak to him during hazing, Ben should have left West Point. Do you agree or not?

16

One in Nine . . .

JACKIE ROBINSON

DO YOU KNOW

1. which of these book titles best fits this story?

BASEBALL SCOUT	BREAKING INTO THE BIG LEAGUES	PEANUTS FOR LUNCH

2. what
   a. young Jackie ate for lunch to fill his stomach?
   b. honor he received after his second year with the Dodgers?

LET'S LOOK AT WORDS.

1. Compound words are two words put together to make one word. *Baseball* is a compound word. It means a game in which you hit a *ball* to get on *base*. Here are five more compound words from the story: *newspapers, schoolboy, basketball, football, shortstop.* Find the two words that were put together to make each compound word. Tell what each separate word means. Tell what each compound word means.

2. Some words have *more* than one meaning. Which of the two meanings below fits *this* story?

Words from the Story	*Meanings*
a. Jackie was a sports <u>star</u>.	shining body in the sky very fine ball player
b. Jackie got his first <u>hit</u>.	knock against ball batted that gets a player on base
c. Jackie worked for a <u>chain</u> of stores.	connected rings many places alike
d. Jackie worked with a <u>track</u> team.	follow sport
e. Jackie heard the yells of the <u>fans</u>.	move air people who love a champion

CAN YOU

1. name four sports in which Jackie starred?
2. tell what honors he received?

WHAT DO YOU THINK?

Once Jackie had joined the Dodgers, it was easy for him to become a star. Do you agree?

17

The Do-It-Yourself Actor...
SIDNEY POITIER

DO YOU KNOW

1. what thing Sidney most wanted to do?
   - *a.* get a job
   - *b.* work on a newspaper
   - *c.* be an actor
   - *d.* play his radio
2. some picture words from the story that make the sentences interesting? Find the words in the story that tell

   a. the kind of
       sunshine Sidney left in Florida
       speakers he listened to on the radio
       hours he spent at hard work
       statue he won in Hollywood

   b. how
       he reached New York
       tall he was

LET'S LOOK AT WORDS.
"Sound-alikes"

Each word in List A sounds like a word in List B. Match the "sound-alikes."

A	B
ad	their
hours	new
weigh	one
won	add
knew	ours
there	way

CAN YOU

choose the best answer?

Sidney Poitier slept on the rooftop because:

1. he liked fresh air
2. he could practice speaking up there
3. he had no place to go
4. he liked to watch the stars

WHAT DO YOU THINK?

1. Could any actor train himself as Sidney did? Explain.
2. Good luck made Sidney an actor. Do you agree?

18

Girl with a Racket . . .

ALTHEA GIBSON

DO YOU KNOW

1. the one thing that Althea's friend told her about sportsmanship?
2. the one dream Althea had all her life?
3. what Althea wrote to tell the world about her dream?

LET'S LOOK AT WORDS.

1. What is the best meaning for the word *tops*, as it is used in *this* story?

Althea was *tops*.

a. **toys**
b. **tents**
c. **best**

2. What is the best meaning for the word *block*, as it is used in this story?

Althea was winner
for her *block*.

a. **part of a street**
b. **child's toy**
c. **shape**

CAN YOU

put these in order? Althea took many steps to the top. In what order did she take these?

    Paddle Tennis Champ of Manhattan
    tennis champ in England
    Paddle Tennis Champ in her block
    college graduate
    National Tennis Champion at Forest Hills, N.Y.
    Paddle Tennis Champ of Harlem

WHAT DO YOU THINK?

1. Althea did not really think the rain was a bad sign for her at Forest Hills. Do you agree?
2. There is something else to real sportsmanship — other than *not getting mad*. What else?

19

A Chance to Speak . . .

MARTIN LUTHER KING, JR.

DO YOU KNOW

1. two things Dr. King did, without guns, to free his people?

2. what a bus boycott means?
3. what right was won by the Negroes through the bus boycott?
4. what the Nobel Peace Prize is?
5. why Dr. King won it?
6. what he did with the money?

LET'S LOOK AT WORDS.

1. Separate each of these compound words into two smaller words:

    without   **something**

2. The "T-word" game. Find pairs of words from the story. The *middle* letter of one word *must* be *the same* as the *first* letter of the other. Examples:

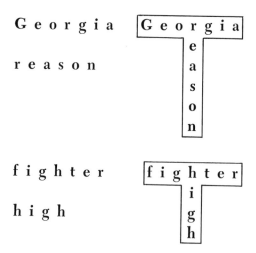

How many "T-words" can you make? Use this list if you wish.

wagons	boycott	buses	college	battles
group	chance	students	leader	true

CAN YOU

pick *two* of these in which you might find something about the Montgomery Bus Boycott?

a. newspapers   *c.* the Holy Bible   *e.* comic books
b. dictionary   *d.* history books

WHAT DO YOU THINK?

Dr. King made up his mind to follow Gandhi's way to free his own people. Was this a good man to follow? Was this a bad man to follow? Why?

20

"Say-Hey"...

WILLIE MAYS

DO YOU KNOW

1. why Aunt Sarah wanted Grandfather to stop teaching baseball to Willie?
2. how to match the words under List A and List B?

A	**B**
the Giants	Willie's aunt
the Birmingham Barons	a Negro team
Sarah	Willie
Leo Durocher	New York team
"Say-Hey Kid"	famous Giant

LET'S LOOK AT WORDS.

1. Separate each of these compound words into two
   smaller words:

   grandfather   **baseball**

2. Here are words from the story. Some have silent letters,
   like *e* in *gave*. Others have double letters, like *tt* in
   batter. Under which heading do these words belong?

Silent Letters			*Double Letters*	
game	home	knew	loved	team
stop	made	yell	presser	became
plate	runner	start	mill	batting
Willie	tease	wanted	them	ball

CAN YOU

put these words under the right headings?

As a Baby	*After High School*	*As a Giant*
ran before he walked	grandfather	Aunt Sarah
All Star Game	fielder in Alabama	Leo Durocher
Birmingham Barons	Most Valuable	train ride to
visit from scout	Player	Minnesota
most exciting player	"Say-Hey Willie"	high pay

WHAT DO YOU THINK?

1. Willie's grandfather could have been left out of this
   story. Do you agree?
2. Willie should have gotten angry when his teammates
   called him "Say-Hey Willie." Do you agree?

INDEX

117